Holidays and Celebrations

Birthdays

by Brenda Haugen
illustrated by Todd Ouren

Thanks to our advisers for their expertise, research, knowledge, and advice:

Alexa Sandmann, Ed.D., Professor of Literacy
The University of Toledo, Toledo, Ohio
Member, National Council for the Social Studies

Susan Kesselring, M.A., Literacy Educator
Rosemount-Apple Valley-Eagan (Minnesota) School District

PICTURE WINDOW BOOKS
MINNEAPOLIS, MINNESOTA

For Grandpa John, my birthday buddy

Managing Editor: Bob Temple
Creative Director: Terri Foley
Editor: Sara E. Hoffmann
Editorial Adviser: Andrea Cascardi
Copy Editor: Laurie Kahn
Designer: Melissa Voda
Page production: The Design Lab
The illustrations in this book were rendered digitally.

Picture Window Books
5115 Excelsior Boulevard
Suite 232
Minneapolis, MN 55416
1-877-845-8392
www.picturewindowbooks.com

Printed in the United States of America.

Library of Congress Cataloging-in-Publication Data
Haugen, Brenda.
Birthdays / written by Brenda Haugen ; illustrated by Todd Ouren.
p. cm. — (Holidays and celebrations)
Summary: Briefly discusses the history and customs connected to
the celebration of birthdays.
Includes bibliographical references.
ISBN 1-4048-0198-7
1. Birthdays—Juvenile literature. [1. Birthdays.] I. Ouren, Todd, ill.
II. Title. III. Holidays and celebrations (Picture Window Books)
GT2430 .H38 2004
394.2—dc21
2003006099

People celebrate their birthdays in many different ways.

Some people spend the day with family.
Some people invite friends to a party and play games.
Some people eat cake and ice cream.

How do you celebrate your birthday?

Rainbows of balloons and streamers
brighten the room.
Friends bring pretty packages,
some tied with colored strings.

A yummy cake is decorated with candles. Everyone sings, "Happy birthday!"

The song "Happy Birthday to You" was written more than 100 years ago! It was composed by two American teachers.

People all around the world celebrate birthdays.

Birthday parties are a special way
of remembering the day you were born.

Long ago, most people
did not have birthday parties.

Sometimes people
wear crowns on their
birthdays. This tradition
started because kings
and queens wore their
crowns to their birthday
celebrations years ago.

Kings and queens celebrated birthdays, but regular people did not.

9

These days, almost everyone celebrates birthdays.

When people throw parties or eat special meals on their birthdays, they are celebrating like kings and queens did long ago.

In some cultures, only children celebrate birthdays. Hindu children celebrate birthdays until they turn 16.

It's fun to get birthday cards in the mail. The tradition of sending birthday cards started in England.

Today, birthday cards are sent in countries all over the world.

In the United States, close to two billion birthday cards are sent each year!

Specially decorated cakes
are tasty birthday treats.
Some of the first
birthday cakes were
made in Germany.
The Germans baked
surprises into the cakes.

Happy Birthday

Thimbles and
coins were some
of the surprises
German children
would find in
their cakes.

In some countries, people still bake surprises into their cakes.

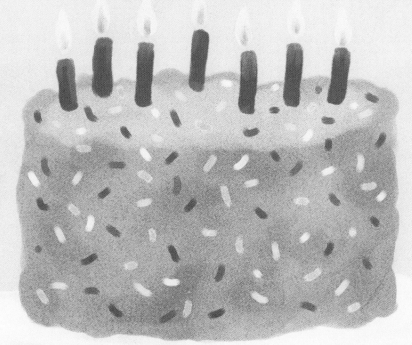

In America, cakes usually do not have surprises inside. Instead, they have fancy decorations on them.

What is that shining brightly
on top of the cake?
Candles!

Candles come in many
pretty colors and shapes.
Some even light up again
after you have blown them out!

When you blow out
your candles, try to do it
in one breath. Many people
believe that if you make
a wish and blow out all
the candles in one breath,
the wish will come true.

Noisemakers are fun birthday-party toys.
They squeak, squawk, and squeal!

Some even have a curled-up paper tube at the end of them. When you blow air into the noisemaker, the tube unrolls and crackles.

Birthdays celebrate your life.
They are a time of joy
for your family and friends.

So blow out your candles,
and make a secret wish.
It's your special day!

When is your birthday? More people have birthdays in August than any other month.

21

You Can Make a Birthday Handprint

What you need:

plaster of paris

water

a large plastic bowl

something to stir the plaster

an aluminum pie plate

a straw

ribbon or yarn

a permanent marker

What you do:

1. Make sure you have an adult to help you.
2. Mix a small amount of plaster of paris with water in the plastic bowl. Stir until the plaster is creamy but stiff. Add more water if you need to do so.
3. Pour the plaster of paris into the pie plate.
4. Place your hand in the plaster to make a handprint.
5. Before the plaster gets hard, use the straw to make a hole about an inch from the top of the mold. Press the straw into the plaster of paris until it touches the bottom of the pie plate. Then remove the straw.
6. Take the plaster out of the pie plate in about 30 minutes, but be careful. It will take about a day for the plaster to dry completely.
7. When the plaster is dry, tie the ribbon or yarn through the hole. You can use this to hang your birthday handprint.
8. Use the permanent marker to write your name and birth date on your birthday handprint.

Remember to make a handprint each year on your birthday. That way, you can see how your hand changes from year to year.

Fun Facts

- Piñatas filled with candy and toys are a favorite part of birthday parties in Mexico. Piñatas come in many shapes, such as animals and flowers. Blindfolded children take turns hitting the piñata with a stick. They try to break the piñata to get the treats inside.

- In Israel, a child gets to sit in a special decorated chair on his or her birthday. Friends and family lift the chair once for each year of the child's life, plus once more for good luck.

- In some Chinese towns, children eat really long noodles on their birthdays. In China, a long noodle is a symbol of a long life.

- The world's largest birthday cake weighed more than 128,000 pounds (58,000 kilograms)! It celebrated the 100th birthday of a city in Alabama.

- In India, children pass out chocolates at school on their birthdays. They also dress in colorful, fancy clothes.

- Russian children have birthday pies instead of birthday cakes.

Words to Know

compose–to write a song

culture–the shared beliefs and customs of a particular group of people

piñata–a colorful decorated container filled with candy and toys. The piñata is hung from the ceiling, and blindfolded children hit it with a stick to break it and make the treats spill out.

symbol–something that stands for something else

thimble–a small cup that fits over a person's finger. It protects a person's finger when he or she is using a needle for sewing.

To Learn More

At the Library

Enderlein, Cheryl L. **Celebrating Birthdays in Russia.**
Mankato, Minn.: Bridgestone Books, 1998.

Hoban, Russell. **A Birthday for Frances.** New York:
HarperCollins, 1995.

Holabird, Katharine. **Angelina's Birthday.** Middleton,
Wis.: Pleasant Company, 2001.

Kindersley, Anabel. **Celebrations!** New York:
DK Pub., 1997.

Fact Hound

Fact Hound offers a safe, fun way to find
Web sites related to this book. All of
the sites on Fact Hound have been
researched by our staff.
http://www.facthound.com

1. Visit the Fact Hound home page.
2. Enter a search word related to this book, or type in
   this special code: 1404801987.
3. Click on the FETCH IT button.

Your trusty Fact Hound will fetch the best sites for you!

Index